giving
thanks
at the table

Compiled by
Elizabeth Hoffman Reed

LITURGY
TRAINING
PUBLICATIONS

GIVING THANKS AT THE TABLE © 1999, Archdiocese of Chicago: Liturgy Training Publications, 1800 North Hermitage Avenue, Chicago IL 60622-1101; 1-800-933-1800, e-mail orders@ltp.org, fax 1-800-933-7094. All rights reserved. See our website at www.ltp.org.

This book was edited by Gabe Huck. Audrey Novak Riley was the production editor. The design is by Anna Manhart, and the typesetting was done by Karen Mitchell in Galliard and Violation. The art is by Susy Pilgrim Waters by Artville. Printed by Printing Arts Chicago.

ISBN 1-56854-257-7

THTBL

contents

praying at meals

Gathering at the table prompts us to give thanks: for all life, for the food, for the time, for the place, for the people.

We need food to live, we need respite and we need companionship. At the table, the hand of God gives all we need. At such a moment we may pray for ourselves, for harmony among those at the table, and for those who have no food or table.

The action of giving thanks goes by several names. We call it "saying grace" and we try to acknowledge in a few words the beauty and the gift symbolized by a meal shared in common. The action is also known as a "blessing." One familiar form goes: "Bless us, O Lord, and these thy gifts, which we are about to receive from thy bounty, through Christ our Lord. Amen." This prayer asks God to be with us at the meal and to be in the food. It also puts us in the humble position of admitting that the food comes from God's abundance, not our own.

Many forms for the table blessing are possible. Everyone at the table can say the same memorized prayer every night. One person can improvise a prayer and say it on behalf of the group and all can say Amen. All may say a verse from the Bible or a psalm that's appropriate for the liturgical season (write it on cards for everybody to see), or all may sing a hymn verse to start the meal (memorize the words). In some households, each person at the table says aloud one thing he or she is thankful for that day.

Many of the meal prayers in this book, especially those for the seasons of the year, invite all present to participate. The best way to do this is to alternate lines or stanzas. Some groups wish to say all the words together and that also works well. These prayers are short enough to be known by heart after praying them regularly for a few weeks.

Singing is always in place at the table. You will find a number of song verses on these pages. When you learn one or more of these by heart, use it to end your meal blessing.

Some households stand to pray, some sit. Some join hands around the table, some fold hands for prayer. Some observe a moment of silence, some make the sign of the cross.

When you welcome guests to your table, let them know how your household blesses the meal gathering, and invite them to join in. Guests are usually honored to be included.

The grace, the table, the food. Our hunger of body and spirit brings us daily to this holy time when we can, if we will, celebrate and strengthen our bonds to one another, to creation and to God. Gunilla Bradde Norris says it this way:

Here is supper. It smells good.
It looks good. It tastes good.
It is good.
All good things come from You.

Let the sweet taste of You
Become the constant blessing
on my tongue.

—EHR

prayers at any meal

Bless us, O Lord,
and these thy gifts
which we are about to receive
from thy bounty,
through Christ our Lord.
Amen.

O thou who clothes the lilies,
who feeds the birds of the sky,
who leads the lambs to pasture
and the deer to the waterside,
who multiplied loaves and fishes
and changed the water to wine:
do thou come to our table
as giver and guest to dine.

God, your people seek shelter,
safe in the warmth of your wings.
They feast at your full table,
slake their thirst in your cool stream,
for you are the fount of life,
you give us light and we see.

— Psalm 36:8b – 10

Blessed are you, Lord,
    God of all creation,
for you feed the whole world
    with your goodness,
with grace, with loving kindness
    and tender mercy.
You give food to all creatures,
and your loving kindness endures forever.
Because of your great goodness
food has never failed us;
O may it not fail us for ever and ever
for the sake of your great name.
You nourish and sustain all creatures
and do good to all.
Blessed are you, O Lord,
    for you give food to all.

—Jewish meal prayer

Blessed are you, Lord,
God of all creation.
Through your goodness
we have this bread,
which earth has given
and human hands have made.

Blessed be God for ever.

Blessed are you, Lord,
God of all creation.
Through your goodness we have this wine,
fruit of the vine and work of human hands.

Blessed be God for ever.

—Roman Rite

Lord Christ,
we ask you to spread our table
    with your mercy.
And may you bless with your gentle hands
the good things you have given us.
We know that whatever we have comes
    from your lavish heart,
for all that is good comes from you.
Thus whatever we eat,
we should give thanks to you.
And having received from your hands,
let us give with equally generous hands
to those who are poor,
breaking bread and sharing our bread
    with them.
For you have told us
that whatever we give to the poor
we give to you.

— Alcuin of York

These texts may be sung to the tune of "Praise God from whom all blessings flow" or another long-meter melody.

Praise God from whom all blessings flow;
Praise God, all creatures here below!
Praise God above, ye heav'nly host,
Praise Father, Son, and Holy Ghost.

Be present at our table, Lord.
Be here and ev'rywhere adored.
Thy creatures bless and grant that we
May feast in paradise with thee.

This text may be sung or recited:
Now thank we all our God
With hearts and hands and voices,
Who wondrous things has done,
In whom this world rejoices,
Who from our mother's arms
Has blessed us on our way
With countless gifts of love
And still is ours today.

At breakfast:
O Lord, shine your love on us each dawn,
and gladden all our days.

Let your loveliness shine on us,
and bless the work we do,
bless the work of our hands.

prayers after a meal

Give food to the hungry, O Lord,
and hunger for you
to those who have food.

Blessed be the Lord
of whose bounty we partake
and by whose goodness we live.

The eyes of all look to you,
you give them food in due time.
You open wide your hand
to feed all living things.

—Psalm 145:15 – 16

god's generosity

God said,
"See, I have given you every plant yielding seed
that is upon the face of all the earth,
and every tree with seed in its fruit;
you shall have them for food.
And to every beast of the earth,
and to every bird of the air,
and to everything that creeps on the earth,
everything that has the breath of life,
I have given every green plant for food."
And it was so.
God saw everything that had been made,
and indeed, it was very good.

— Genesis 1:29 – 31

sunday prayers

*Any blessing for a season or for Ordinary Time
may be used. Begin and end in a way unique to the
Lord's Day:*

At the beginning of any blessing:
Let us give thanks to the Lord our God.
It is right to give God thanks and praise.

At the conclusion of any blessing:
The Lord bless us and keep us.
Amen.

The Lord's face shine upon us
and be gracious to us.
Amen.

The Lord look upon us with kindness
and give us peace.
Amen.

the lord's day

The whole of Sunday becomes a great school of charity, justice and peace. The presence of the Risen Lord in the midst of his people becomes an undertaking of solidarity, a compelling force for inner renewal, an inspiration to change the structures of sin in which individuals, communities and at times entire peoples are entangled. Far from being an escape, the Christian Sunday is a prophecy inscribed on time itself, a prophecy obliging the faithful to follow in the footsteps of the One who came "to preach good news to the poor, to proclaim release to captives and new sight to the blind, to set at liberty those who are oppressed, and to proclaim the acceptable year of the Lord" (Luke 4:18—19).

—**John Paul II**, *Dies Domini*

friday prayer

The Catholic bishops of the United States have urged all Catholics to observe Friday as a day of penance and prayer for peace. Friday fasting and abstinence has for centuries been part of Catholic life. Fasting means eating less food, perhaps even not eating some meals. Abstinence means not eating certain foods at all.

On Friday, except during the Easter season:

All praise be yours, God our Creator,
as we wait in joyful hope
for the flowering of justice
and the fullness of peace.
All praise for this day, this Friday.
By our weekly fasting and prayer,
cast out the spirit of war,
of fear and mistrust,
and make us grow hungry
for human kindness,
thirsty for solidarity
with all the people of your dear earth.
May all our prayer, our fasting,
and our deeds be done
in the name of Jesus.
Amen.

fasting

Is this not the fast I choose:
to loose the bonds of injustice,
to undo the thongs of the yoke,
to let the oppressed go free
and to break every yoke?
Is it not to share your bread with the hungry,
and bring the homeless poor into your house;
when you see the naked, to cover them,
and not to hide yourself from your own kin?

— Isaiah 58:6 – 7

Fasting is the soul of prayer,
mercy is the lifeblood of fasting.
If we have not all three together,
we have nothing.

— Peter Chrysologus

While fasting with the body, brothers and sisters,
let us also fast in spirit.
Let us loose every bond of iniquity;
let us undo the knots of every contract
made by violence;
let us tear up all unjust agreements;
let us give bread to the hungry
and welcome to our house
the poor who have no roof to cover them,
that we may receive mercy from Christ our God.

— **Byzantine vespers**

advent

Before the meal (all together or alternating):
Come, Lord Jesus!
Come quickly!

Blessed are you, Lord, God of all creation,
in the darkness and in the light.

Blessed are you
in this food and in our sharing.

Blessed are you
as we wait in joyful hope
for the coming of our Savior, Jesus Christ.

For the kingdom, the power and the glory
are yours, now and forever. Amen.

After the meal:

The eyes of all creatures
look with hope to you, O Lord.

And you give them their food
in due season.

christmas season

Before the meal (all together or alternating):
Christ is born for us!
Come, let us adore.

Lord Jesus,
in the peace of this season
our spirits rejoice.
With the animals and the angels,
with the shepherds and the stars,
with Mary and Joseph
we sing God's praise.
By your coming
may the hungry be filled with good things
and may our table and home be blessed.

Glory to God in the highest!
And peace to God's people on earth.

After the meal:
The Word became flesh, alleluia!
And dwelt among us, alleluia!

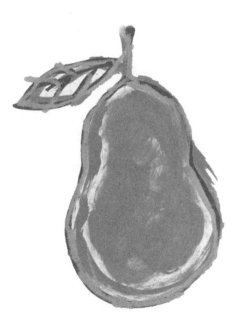

feasting

A cheerful heart has a continual feast.
Better a little with the fear of the Lord
than great treasure and trouble with it.
Better is a dinner of vegetables where love is
than a fatted ox and hatred with it.

— Proverbs 15:15 – 17

O Lord, refresh our sensibilities. Give us this day our daily taste. Restore to us soups that spoons will not sink in, and sauces which are never the same twice. Raise up among us stews with more gravy than we have bread to blot it with, and casseroles that put starch and substance in our limp modernity. Take away our fear of fat, and make us glad of the oil which ran upon Aaron's beard. Give us pasta with a hundred fillings, and rice in a thousand variations. Above all, give us grace . . . to fast till we come to a refreshed sense of what we have and then to dine gratefully on all that comes to hand. Drive far from us, O Most Bountiful, the demons that possess us; deliver us from the fear of calories and the bondage of nutrition; and set us free once more in our own land, where we shall serve thee as thou hast blessed us — with the dew of heaven, the fatness of the earth, and plenty of corn and wine. Amen.

— Robert Farrar Capon

winter

Before the meal (all together or alternating):
How good to sing God praise!
How lovely the sound!

The Lord feeds the cattle
and young ravens when they call.
The Lord favors the reverent,
those who trust in God's mercy.

The Lord fills your land with peace,
giving you golden wheat.

The Lord sends heavy snow
and scatters frost like ashes.
God speaks, the ice melts;
God breathes, the streams flow.

—Psalm 147:1, 9, 11, 14, 16, 18

Sing to "Praise God from whom all blessings flow"
or another tune of this meter:
Dear Lord of wintertime, we bless
Your name with cheer and thankfulness.
At welcome table all are fed:
Give us to share our daily bread.

After the meal:
Lord, hear the longing of the poor,
listen to their every word,
and give them heart.
Then the orphaned and oppressed
will gain justice.

—Psalm 10:17–18a

lent

Behold! Now is the acceptable time.
Now is the day of salvation.

I was hungry.
And you gave me food.

I was thirsty.
And you gave me drink.

I was a stranger.
And you welcomed me.

I was naked.
And you clothed me.

I was ill.
And you cared for me.

I was in jail.
And you visited me.

page 28

Lord Jesus Christ,
may our lenten fasting
turn us toward all our brothers and sisters
who are in need.
Bless us all in the sharing of your gifts.
Send us through Lent with good cheer,
and bring us at last
to the all-embracing joy of Easter.
Amen.

After the meal:
Not on bread alone are we to live.
But on every word
that comes from the mouth of God.

fasting

The merit of a fast day is in the charity dispensed then.

— The Talmud

Let us fast in such a way that we lavish our lunches upon the poor, so that we may not store up in our purses what we intended to eat, but rather in the stomachs of the poor.

— Caesarius of Arles

Whenever you fast, do not look dismal, like the hypocrites, for they disfigure their faces so as to show others they are fasting. Truly I tell you, they have received their reward. But when you fast, put oil on your head and wash your face, so that your fasting may be seen not by others but by your Father who is in secret; and your Father who sees in secret will reward you.

— Matthew 6:16–18

*Fasting is a medicine. But like all medicines,
though it be very profitable to the person who
knows how to use it, it frequently becomes
useless (and even harmful) in the hands of
those who are unskillful in its use.*

—John Chrysostom

*Mercy is to fasting as rain is to the earth.
However much you may cultivate your heart,
clear the soil of your nature, root out your
vices and sow virtues, if you do not release the
springs of mercy, your fasting will not bear
fruit. When you fast, a thin sowing of mercy
will mean a thin harvest. When you fast, what
you pour out in mercy overflows into your
barn. So do not lose by saving, but gather in
by scattering.*

—Peter Chrysologus

the triduum

*From Holy Thurday evening until the great Vigil
in the night between Holy Saturday and Easter,
the catechumens and the baptized fast and pray and
await the celebration of baptism. Any meals are
very simple. "Let the paschal fast be kept sacred. Let
it be observed everywhere on Good Friday and,
where possible, prolonged throughout Holy Saturday,
as a way of coming to the joys of the Sunday of the
resurrection with uplifted and welcoming heart."
(Constitution on the Sacred Liturgy, 110) The same
prayer is used before and after meals.*

For our sake Christ was obedient,
accepting even death, death on a cross.

Therefore God raised him on high
and gave him the name
above all other names.

the paschal fast

Through greed we underwent
the first stripping,
overcome by the bitter tasting of the fruit,
and we became exiles from God.
But let us turn back to repentance and,
fasting from the food that gives us pleasure,
let us cleanse our senses
on which the enemy makes war.
Let us strengthen our hearts
with the hope of grace,
and not with foods which brought no benefit
to those who trusted in them.
Our food shall be the Lamb of God
on the holy and radiant night
of his Awakening.

— Byzantine vespers

easter season

Before the meal (all together or alternating):
We have put on Christ, alleluia!
In Christ we have been baptized, alleluia!

This is the day the Lord has made.
Let us rejoice and be glad in it.

Joyfully do we praise you,
Lord Jesus Christ, risen from the grave.
Remain here in our midst
as we share these gifts.
May we receive you as a guest
in all our brothers and sisters
and be welcomed by you
to share the feast of your Spirit,
for you live and reign for ever and ever.
Amen. Alleluia!

After the meal:
Lord, send out your Spirit.
And renew the face of the earth.
Alleluia!

feasting

*Day by day, as they spent much time together
in the temple, they broke bread at home and
ate their food with glad and generous hearts,
praising God and having the goodwill of all
the people.*

— Acts 2:46 – 47

*Each thing I have received, from thee it came.
Each thing for which I hope,
from thy love it will come.
Each thing I enjoy, it is of thy bounty.
Each thing I ask comes of thy disposing.*

— Celtic prayer

You spread a table before me
as my foes look on.
You soothe my head with oil;
my cup is more than full.

— Psalm 23:5

Why do you spend your money
for that which is not bread,
and your wages
for that which does not satisfy?
Listen carefully to me, and eat what is good,
and delight yourselves in rich fare.

— Isaiah 55:2

summer

Before the meal (all together or alternating):
I will bless you, Lord my God!
You fill the world with awe.
You nourish the earth
with what you create.

You make grass grow for cattle,
make plants grow for people,
food to eat from the earth
and wine to warm the heart,
oil to glisten on faces
and bread for bodily strength.

All look to you for food
when they hunger;
you provide it and they feed.
You open your hand, they feast;
the face of the earth comes alive.

—Psalm 104:1, 13b–15, 27–28, 30

Sing to "Praise God from whom all blessings flow"
or another tune of this meter:
Around this table, may the Lord
Be ever and always adored,
The weary find a welcome rest,
And all who suffer want be blessed!

After the meal:
We give you thanks for all your gifts,
almighty God, living and reigning
now and for ever.
Amen.

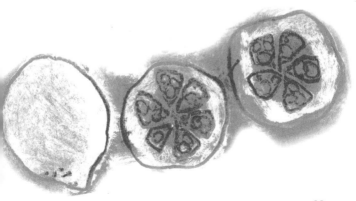

autumn

Before the meal (all together or alternating):
Praise is yours, God in Zion.
Happy are those you invite
and then welcome to your courts.
Fill us with the plenty of your house,
the holiness of your temple.

You tend and water the land.
How wonderful the harvest!

You crown the year with riches.
All you touch comes alive:
untilled lands yield crops,
hills are dressed in joy,

flocks clothe the pastures,
valleys wrap themselves in grain.
They all shout for joy
and break into song.

—Psalm 65:2, 5, 10, 12–14

Sing to "Praise God from whom all blessings flow"
or another tune of this meter:

O Lord of harvest, glory be
In autumn's fruitful majesty!
For ev'ry blessing earth displays
We offer you our grateful praise.

After the meal:

The land delivers its harvest,
God, our God, has blessed us.

O God, continue your blessing,
may the whole world worship you.

Psalm 67:7 – 8

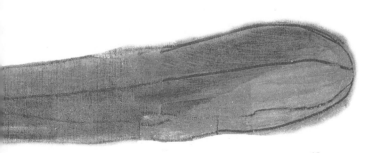

the giver of all good gifts

We cannot love God unless we love each other,
and to love each other we must know each
other in the breaking of the bread and we are
not alone any more. . . . Heaven is a
banquet and life is a banquet, too, even with
a crust, where there is companionship. Love
comes with community.

— Dorothy Day

Jesus said, "When you give a luncheon or a
dinner, do not invite your friends or your
brothers or your relatives or rich neighbors, in
case they may invite you in return, and you
would be repaid. But when you give a banquet,
invite the poor, the crippled, the lame, and
the blind. And you will be blessed, because they
cannot repay you, for you will be repaid at the
resurrection of the righteous."

— Luke 14:12–14

Every mealtime fills Christians with gratitude for the living, present Lord and God, Jesus Christ. Not that they seek any morbid spiritualization of material gifts; on the contrary, Christians, in their wholehearted joy in the good gifts of this physical life, acknowledge their Lord as the true giver of all good gifts, and beyond this, as the true gift, the true bread of life itself; and finally as the one who is calling them to the banquet of the kingdom of God.

— **Dietrich Bonhoeffer**

praise and gratitude

The meal is surrounded with other moments, tasks, necessities. They too are important. In a society that thrives on fast food and disposable utensils, there's little space for reverence and wonder before the marvelous thing it is to eat. Downgrading the preparation, eliminating the clean-up, we cheapen the very acts of eating and being together.

In our tradition it is not only important to be grateful, it is essential. The tradition is praise and gratitude. That is a way of living day after day. At certain moments it seeks expression, moments that are turning points of our ordinary lives: the morning, the evening, going to bed, and our meals. We are people of the table, people who know the Lord in the breaking of the bread, people who know fasting and feasting as religious, world-shaping deeds.

The prayer of the table becomes a habit — not that it is done without thought, but simply: This is how we do things. Its strength depends not on the schedules and upsets of the given day but on the way we habitually come to table. What is the preparation of the food like? How is it shared? How are foods selected? If there is the luxury of choice, where in our choice is responsibility (to farmworkers who may be asking us to boycott certain products, to the world, mostly hungry, that could never support a population that ate meat in the quantities we do)? If there are hard times, can we find gratitude for the beans and rice that are forever the food of the poor? The growing and the buying and the storing and the cutting and mixing and cooking and the serving of food are vital, lovely acts that are eaten at table.

Then there is the table itself and its preparation, also a shared task. The vessels of the table should be treated as the vessels of the altar, Saint Benedict wrote in his rule for monasteries in the sixth century. They hold for us the fruit of the earth. However simple, the plates and napkins and utensils and serving bowls and pitchers of the table are to be cared for, honored. There is no place for clutter or display. The cleaning up is as important as the setting. These moments are not solemn any more than they are burdensome, but simply filled with the sense that here is what being a Christian household is finally about. And that is good.

In all of this and especially in the choice of a prayer for a given meal, there is the variety of our circumstances. We have good days and bad, calm days with leisure to visit and linger at the table and days when we are on the run. In the family, it is the usual way that is important, not the all-too-frequent exceptions. Sometimes all cannot be there: Yet there can still be a meal together for those who are. The moment of prayer is no less important when the household is two or one.

Food and people in communion are, Sunday by Sunday, the very way Christians express themselves, become themselves. That eucharist's whole being and strength depend on the way such communion happens around all the tables of all the people.

— Gabe Huck